Killer Technique®: Fiddle

by Suzanna Barnes

© 2012 BY MEL BAY PUBLICATIONS, INC., PACIFIC, MO 63069.
ALL RIGHTS RESERVED. INTERNATIONAL COPYRIGHT SECURED. B.M.I. MADE AND PRINTED IN U.S.A.
No part of this publication may be reproduced in whole or in part, or stored in a retrieval system, or transmitted in any form
or by any means, electronic, mechanical, photocopy, recording, or otherwise, without written permission of the publisher.

Visit us on the Web at www.melbay.com — E-mail us at email@melbay.com

Table of Contents

Introduction 3

Left-Hand Workout 4

Finger Patterns 4

Finger Orderings 5

Bowing Workout 8

Bowing Patterns and Bowing Pattern Alternates 8

2 String Combinations 9

3 String Combinations 10

4 String Combinations 12

Combining Workouts 15

About the Author 17

Introduction

The **Killer Technique**® series has been designed to give aspiring musicians answers to common questions in a brief, affordable, yet informative fashion, and is now available for fiddle players! *Killer Technique*® provides concepts and daily routines to help players get more control over their instrument by improving their technique and avoiding injury.

This book has been adapted from Corey Christiansen's guitar book Gig Savers: Killer Technique (MB# 20028). The writing, concepts and exercises found in his book remain intact, except in places where I felt changes were needed to better suit the instrument and where I considered it beneficial to include supplementary information.

Having good, efficient technique is paramount in becoming a great violinist in any genre. By improving technique, a violinist can do more by working less. Many of the exercises in this book are very basic and may seem simple at first, but get harder. Even the easiest exercises, played perfectly, can be challenging for an experienced violinist. The idea is to take these workouts slowly. By doing so, proper technique will be acquired and hand injury will be avoided.

It is a constant battle to synchronize bowing technique with the left hand. If it were easy, everybody would be able to play the violin at a high level. Many violinists have found success in building technique by working on the left hand and bowing separately. If a new technique is being worked on to develop bowing technique, make the exercises easy for the left hand in the beginning. If a technique is being worked on for left-hand development, make the bowing relatively easy. As the level of technique increases, what used to be challenging will become easy for both hands. Before long, concepts that were previously hard for the right hand will be easy material used to supplement an exercise that is difficult for the left hand. It will be apparent which hand is being worked in each of the exercises. Hopefully, each violinist will use these ideas as a springboard to create workouts of their own. Constructing workouts can be a never-ending project. The trick is to find a methodical way to create and stay organized.

The exercises in this book are not written in standard notation. The patterns that make up the exercises are written with finger pattern diagrams, finger order numbers, string numbers, fingerboard diagrams and bowing patterns. This will allow violinists, regardless of reading abilities, of all styles and all levels, to use the exercises.

Left-Hand Workout

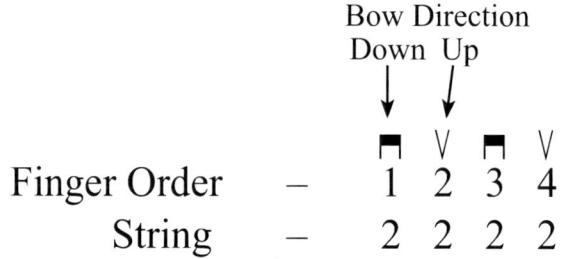

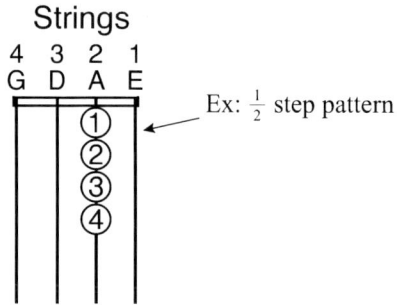

Shown below are 16 finger patterns that can be chosen from when doing your left-hand exercises. All of these patterns use fingers 1-4 and are within the distance of an augmented fourth. Please practice with caution, as some of these may be a stretch.

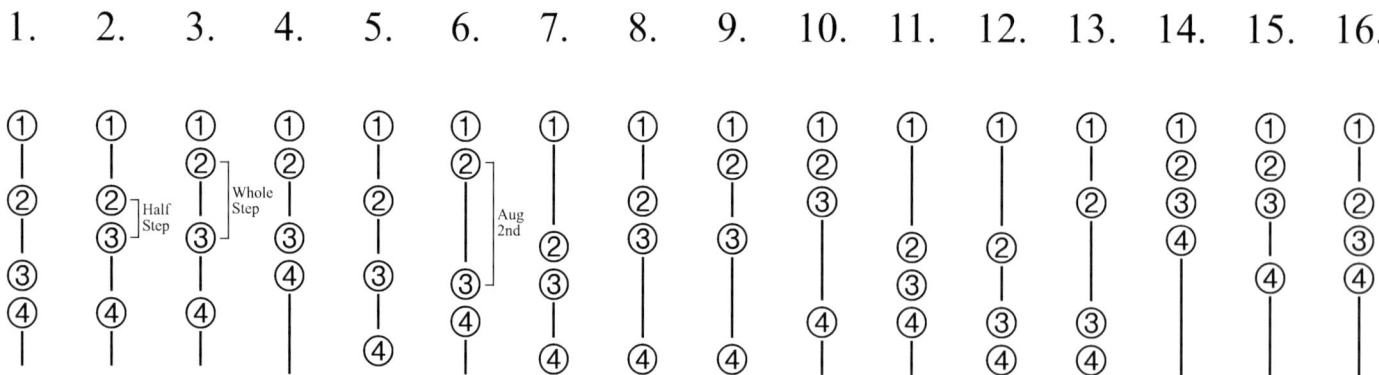

Exercises:

To create your exercise, choose one finger pattern from above to combine with one of the following permutations or finger orderings of 1-2-3-4.

1.	1-2-3-4	7.	2-1-3-4	13.	3-1-2-4	19.	4-1-2-3
2.	1-2-4-3	8.	2-1-4-3	14.	3-1-4-2	20.	4-1-3-2
3.	1-3-2-4	9.	2-3-1-4	15.	3-2-1-4	21.	4-2-1-3
4.	1-3-4-2	10.	2-3-4-1	16.	3-2-4-1	22.	4-2-3-1
5.	1-4-2-3	11.	2-4-1-3	17.	3-4-1-2	23.	4-3-1-2
6.	1-4-3-2	12.	2-4-3-1	18.	3-4-2-1	24.	4-3-2-1

After placing your hand with the first finger at the note F natural on the E string (string 1), play the finger pattern/finger order pairing using separate bows at a moderately slow tempo. Then move it straight across the fingerboard crossing from the strings E-A-D-G, and then back from G-D-A-E. DO NOT change the direction of the pattern when the string order is reversed. You can also use 2 or 4 notes to a bow, but let your focus remain on left hand accuracy.

Example:

Finger order no. 1:	1-2-3-4	1-2-3-4	1-2-3-4	1-2-3-4
String:	1-1-1-1	2-2-2-2	3-3-3-3	4-4-4-4

Reverse String Order

Finger order no. 1:	1-2-3-4	1-2-3-4	1-2-3-4	1-2-3-4
String:	4-4-4-4	3-3-3-3	2-2-2-2	1-1-1-1

Since each of these patterns are 'closed', meaning that no open strings are used, they are then moveable and can be played starting on any note in any position. A typical workout could be played from strings E-A-D-G and then moved up a half step and continued with strings G-D-A-E, and so on.

Example:

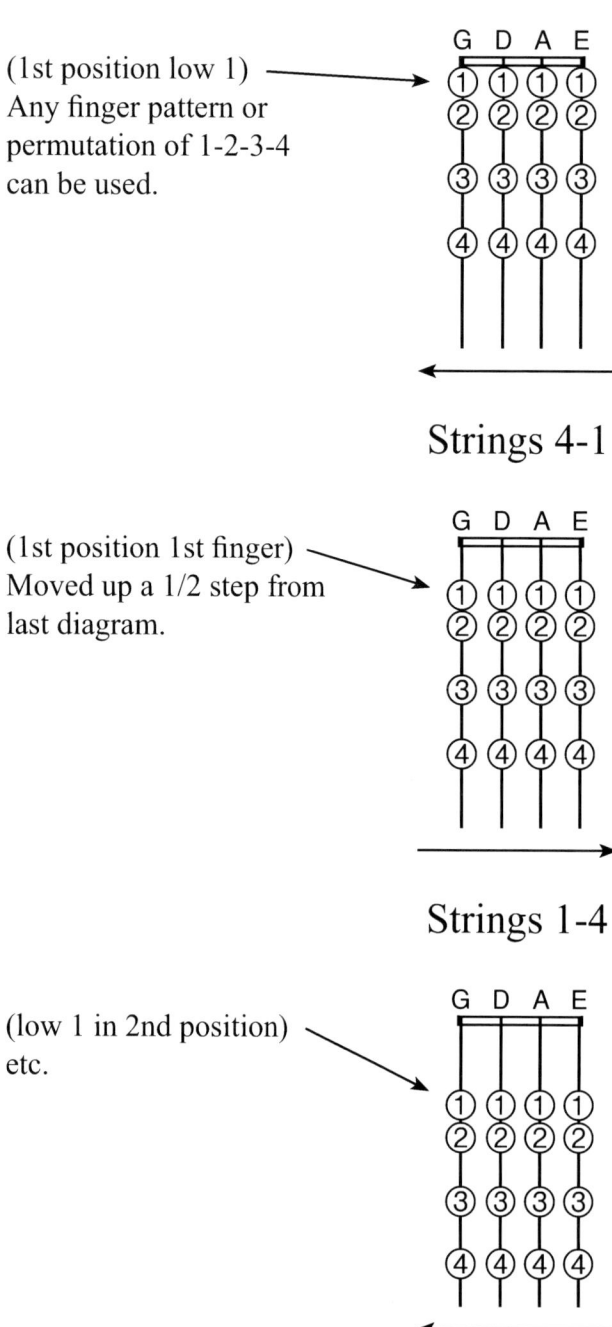

Strings 1-4

(1st position low 1) — Any finger pattern or permutation of 1-2-3-4 can be used.

Strings 4-1

(1st position 1st finger) — Moved up a 1/2 step from last diagram.

Strings 1-4

(low 1 in 2nd position) etc.

    Continue this half step movement up the neck and once you reach 7th position and have played the pattern starting on the octave of each of your open strings, you can work your way down the neck by descending in a similar half-step manner.

    If a fluid half-step movement is too difficult, allow yourself a break to set up your fingers and find your notes before you begin in the new position. On the other hand, if you are looking for more challenging ways to move these patterns around the fingerboard, consider moving by distances of specific intervals such as minor thirds.

    In all cases, you want to achieve clear tone and good intonation. Depending on which finger pattern and ordering you choose, it can become difficult to navigate your way up and down the neck. Use your ear and try to identify the note you are on and make sure you haven't altered the pattern at any point. This can become a great ear training exercise as well as technique building. Also, it would be beneficial to isolate any problem area and work on that limited figure before returning to an exercise. For example, let's say you are having trouble going from your third finger to your fourth finger with good intonation. Isolate these two fingers and practice this pattern across all four strings.

Example:

Finger order:	3-4	3-4	3-4	3-4	Repeat Down and Up
String:	1-1	1-1	1-1	1-1	All Four Strings

Every exercise should be played slowly and perfectly before playing it fast. Also, each note should get the same amount of time. This means that the rhythm for each note is equal and should be steady. If practicing with a metronome, each note can get a beat, a half a beat, or a quarter of a beat. The goal is to able to rip through the exercise flawlessly, but accurate speed will not come without mastering these exercises at a relatively slow speed at first.

You can create your own exercises by forming your own finger patterns/orderings. Perhaps you'd like to repeat a note or add a note with a slide in your pattern. Here's an example:

Original: Changed to:

Considerations and Options: In the above example, you may want to consider if you'd like to use a single stroke to cover the slide from 2-2, or if you'd like to bow each note separately. Also, if playing with a metronome set in a duple meter, you may want to alter the rhythm, playing the 5-note pattern as a quintuplet. Another option could be to repeat a note, creating a pattern of 6 notes and then perhaps changing to triple meter on your metronome.

The point of practicing in this manner is to exhaust your options and possibilities so that when it comes time to play, you're ready for anything. By doing these exercises, you can build strength and increase agility in your left hand and fingers. The exercises can also help build and maintain muscle memory. Many of the finger patterns are extracted from major, minor, diminished, and whole-tone scales and by practicing inside these common shapes, you will obtain a foundation that can help in the execution of any similar movements as they occur in your repertoire. Also, you will start to gain familiarity with the fingerboard and neck and become more comfortable playing in any position.

Bowing Workout

In the following exercises, you will choose to combine different bowing patterns with various 2, 3, or 4 note string combinations. These exercises use only open strings in the beginning. Correct usage of your wrist and bow arm is crucial to your success at these exercises and I highly recommend playing in front of a mirror so that you can check up on your technique. Some tips I may offer would be to notice and feel the different levels of your bow arm that are needed for smooth string crossings. Also, when alternating between strings, use rotation of your wrist to help guide your bow. Lastly, try to eliminate any unnecessary arm movement.

You can practice these exercises to try and reach a point of bowing fluidity and ease at high speeds or you can practice them simply to get used to different patterns and string crossings. Feel free to add any articulations or accents to your patterns like staccato, legato, marcato, tenuto, etc. You may also want to practice playing your patterns in isolated parts of the bow.

To begin, choose one of the following bowing patterns (bowing alternates are needed for certain exercises), and combine it with a 2, 3, or 4 string combination also listed below and begin at a comfortable speed. Repeat exercises as necessary before moving on.

Bowing Patterns

Bowing Pattern Alternates

2 String Combinations

1.
Finger order: ‖: 0-0-0-0   0-0-0-0 | 0-0-0-0   0-0-0-0 | 0-0-0-0   0-0-0-0 :‖
String: 2-1-2-1   2-1-2-1 | 3-2-3-2   3-2-3-2 | 4-3-4-3   4-3-4-3

2.
Finger order: ‖: 0-0-0-0   0-0-0-0 | 0-0-0-0   0-0-0-0 | 0-0-0-0   0-0-0-0 :‖
String: 1-2-1-2   1-2-1-2 | 2-3-2-3   2-3-2-3 | 3-4-3-4   3-4-3-4

3.
Finger order: ‖: 0-0-0-0   0-0-0-0 | 0-0-0-0   0-0-0-0 :‖   alternate bowings needed for the bowing patterns ② through ⑧
String: 3-1-3-1   3-1-3-1 | 4-2-4-2   4-2-4-2

4.
Finger order: ‖: 0-0-0-0   0-0-0-0 | 0-0-0-0   0-0-0-0 :‖   alternate bowings needed for the bowing patterns ② through ⑧
String: 1-3-1-3   1-3-1-3 | 2-4-2-4   2-4-2-4

5.
Finger order: ‖: 0-0-0-0   0-0-0-0 :‖   alternate bowings needed for the bowing patterns ② through ⑧
String: 4-1-4-1   4-1-4-1

6.
Finger order: ‖: 0-0-0-0   0-0-0-0 :‖   alternate bowings needed for the bowing patterns ② through ⑧
String: 1-4-1-4   1-4-1-4

Just as we had the option of altering the left-hand patterns in any way, you can also alter a string-pattern. In the following example, I have altered number 1 of the 2-string bowing patterns by doubling the A string (string 2) each time it came up. I then added accents and made the pattern fit within a two bar phrase in duple meter. This can be played between strings 3 and 2 as well as between strings 4 and 3.

‖: ⊓ V ⊓ V ⊓ V ⊓ V | ⊓ V ⊓ V ⊓ V ⊓ V :‖
    2 2 1 2 2 1 2 2   1 2 2 1 2 2 1 2

(accents > on beats as shown)

3 String Combinations

7.
Finger order: 0-0-0-0   0-0-0-0   0-0-0-0   0-0-0-0
String: 3-2-1-2   3-2-1-2   4-3-2-3   4-3-2-3

8.
Finger order: 0-0-0-0   0-0-0-0   0-0-0-0   0-0-0-0
String: 1-2-3-2   1-2-3-2   2-3-4-3   2-3-4-3

9.
Finger order: 0-0-0-0   0-0-0-0   0-0-0-0   0-0-0-0
String: 3-1-2-1   3-1-2-1   4-2-3-2   4-2-3-2

10.
Finger order: 0-0-0-0   0-0-0-0   0-0-0-0   0-0-0-0
String: 1-3-2-3   1-3-2-3   2-4-3-4   2-4-3-4

alternate bowings needed for bowing patterns ②, ⑤, ⑦ & ⑧

11.
Finger order: 0-0-0-0   0-0-0-0   0-0-0-0   0-0-0-0
String: 2-1-3-1   2-1-3-1   3-2-4-2   3-2-4-2

12.
Finger order: 0-0-0-0   0-0-0-0   0-0-0-0   0-0-0-0
String: 2-3-1-3   2-3-1-3   3-4-2-4   3-4-2-4

alternate bowings needed for bowing patterns ④ through ⑧

13.
Finger order: 0-0-0-0   0-0-0-0
String: 4-2-1-2   4-2-1-2

alternate bowings needed for bowing patterns ②, ④, ⑤, ⑦ & ⑧

14.
Finger order: 0-0-0-0   0-0-0-0
String: 1-2-4-2   1-2-4-2

alternate bowings needed for bowing patterns ③ through ⑧

15.
Finger order: 0-0-0-0   0-0-0-0
String: 4-1-2-1   4-1-2-1

alternate bowings needed for bowing patterns ② and ④ through ⑧

16.
Finger order: ‖: 0-0-0-0   0-0-0-0 :‖   use alternate bowings for ② through ⑧
String: 1-4-2-4   1-4-2-4

17.
Finger order: ‖: 0-0-0-0   0-0-0-0 :‖   use alternate bowings for ③ through ⑧
String: 2-1-4-1   2-1-4-1

18.
Finger order: ‖: 0-0-0-0   0-0-0-0 :‖   use alternate bowings for ② through ⑧
String: 2-4-1-4   2-4-1-4

19.
Finger order: ‖: 0-0-0-0   0-0-0-0 :‖   use alternate bowings for ③ through ⑧
String: 4-3-1-3   4-3-1-3

20.
Finger order: ‖: 0-0-0-0   0-0-0-0 :‖   use alternate bowings for ②,⑤,⑦ & ⑧
String: 1-3-4-3   1-3-4-3

21.
Finger order: ‖: 0-0-0-0   0-0-0-0 :‖   use alternate bowings for ② through ⑧
String: 4-1-3-1   4-1-3-1

22.
Finger order: ‖: 0-0-0-0   0-0-0-0 :‖   use alternate bowings for ②,⑦ & ⑧
String: 1-4-3-4   1-4-3-4

23.
Finger order: ‖: 0-0-0-0   0-0-0-0 :‖   use alternate bowings for ② through ⑧
String: 3-1-4-1   3-1-4-1

24.
Finger order: ‖: 0-0-0-0   0-0-0-0 :‖   use alternate bowings for ③ through ⑧
String: 3-4-1-4   3-4-1-4

4 String Combinations

25.
Finger order: ‖: 0-0-0-0   0-0-0-0 :‖
String: 1-2-3-4   1-2-3-4

26.
Finger order: ‖: 0-0-0-0   0-0-0-0 :‖   use alternate bowings for ④,⑥,⑦ & ⑧
String: 1-2-4-3   1-2-4-3

27.
Finger order: ‖: 0-0-0-0   0-0-0-0 :‖   use alternate bowings for ②,③, and ⑤ through ⑧
String: 1-3-2-4   1-3-2-4

28.
Finger order: ‖: 0-0-0-0   0-0-0-0 :‖   use alternate bowings for ②,③, and ⑤ through ⑧
String: 1-3-4-2   1-3-4-2

29.
Finger order: ‖: 0-0-0-0   0-0-0-0 :‖   use alternate bowings for ② and ④ through ⑧
String: 1-4-2-3   1-4-2-3

30.
Finger order: ‖: 0-0-0-0   0-0-0-0 :‖   use alternate bowings for ②,⑤,⑦ & ⑧
String: 1-4-3-2   1-4-3-2

31.
Finger order: ‖: 0-0-0-0   0-0-0-0 :‖   use alternate bowings for ④ and ⑥ through ⑧
String: 2-1-3-4   2-1-3-4

32.
Finger order: ‖: 0-0-0-0   0-0-0-0 :‖   use alternate bowings for ④ and ⑥ through ⑧
String: 2-1-4-3   2-1-4-3

33.
Finger order: ‖: 0-0-0-0   0-0-0-0 :‖   use alternate bowings for ③
String: 2-3-1-4   2-3-1-4   through ⑧

34.
Finger order: ‖: 0-0-0-0   0-0-0-0 :‖   use alternate bowings for ③,⑤,⑥
String: 2-3-4-1   2-3-4-1   & ⑧

35.
Finger order: ‖: 0-0-0-0   0-0-0-0 :‖   use alternate bowings for ②
String: 2-4-1-3   2-4-1-3   through ⑧

36.
Finger order: ‖: 0-0-0-0   0-0-0-0 :‖   use alternate bowings for ②,③,
String: 2-4-3-1   2-4-3-1   and ⑤ through ⑧

37.
Finger order: ‖: 0-0-0-0   0-0-0-0 :‖   use alternate bowings for ②,③,⑤
String: 3-1-2-4   3-1-2-4   & ⑧

38.
Finger order: ‖: 0-0-0-0   0-0-0-0 :‖   use alternate bowings for ②
String: 3-1-4-2   3-1-4-2   through ⑧

39.
Finger order: ‖: 0-0-0-0   0-0-0-0 :‖   use alternate bowings for ③,⑤,⑥
String: 3-2-1-4   3-2-1-4   & ⑧

40.
Finger order: ‖: 0-0-0-0   0-0-0-0 :‖   use alternate bowings for ③
String: 3-2-4-1   3-2-4-1   through ⑧

41.
Finger order: |: 0-0-0-0 0-0-0-0 :| use alternate bowings for ④ and ⑥
String: 3-4-1-2   3-4-1-2   through ⑧

42.
Finger order: |: 0-0-0-0 0-0-0-0 :| use alternate bowings for ④ and ⑥
String: 3-4-2-1   3-4-2-1   through ⑧

43.
Finger order: |: 0-0-0-0 0-0-0-0 :| use alternate bowings for ②,⑤,⑦
String: 4-1-2-3   4-1-2-3   & ⑧

44.
Finger order: |: 0-0-0-0 0-0-0-0 :| use alternate bowings for ② and ④
String: 4-1-3-2   4-1-3-2   through ⑧

45.
Finger order: |: 0-0-0-0 0-0-0-0 :| use alternate bowings for ②,③, and
String: 4-2-1-3   4-2-1-3   ⑤ through ⑧

46.
Finger order: |: 0-0-0-0 0-0-0-0 :| use alternate bowings for ②,③, and
String: 4-2-3-1   4-2-3-1   ⑤ through ⑧

47.
Finger order: |: 0-0-0-0 0-0-0-0 :| use alternate bowings for ④ and ⑥
String: 4-3-1-2   4-3-1-2   through ⑧

48.
Finger order: |: 0-0-0-0 0-0-0-0 :|
String: 4-3-2-1   4-3-2-1

Combining Workouts

To create more exercises for further technical development, combine the exercises presented for the left hand with the bowing exercises. This is where the real fun begins. A sample exercise is shown below.

Finger Pattern: #3 (①②—③—④)

Finger Order: #13 (3-1-2-4)

String Combo: #1 (‖: 2-1-2-1   2-1-2-1 | 3-2-3-2   3-2-3-2 | 4-3-4-3   4-3-4-3 :‖)

Bowing Pattern: #2 (‖: ♫. ♪ ♪ | ♫. ♪ ♪ :‖)

On the fingerboard, the exercise looks like this:

(play each pattern twice)

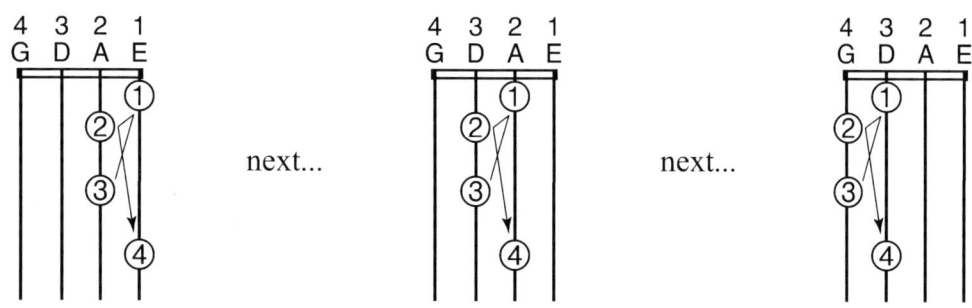

Written out, the exercise looks like this:

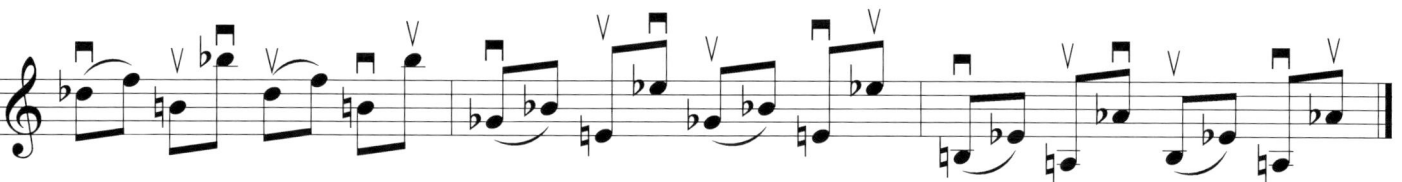

Another exercise can be formed by combining your left hand pattern/ordering with a bowing pattern and then working it up and down the neck in half-steps on a single string, therefore leaving out the string combinations.

I hope the ideas and exercises presented in this book will help spur your own alterations, creations, and discoveries. Your technique and creativity will then work hand in hand, challenging and giving momentum to one another. With the many possibilities available, search out the ones that stimulate and challenge you and master them.

About the Author

Suzanna has been playing music almost all of her life. She started when she was just three years old on the violin and continues to this day. Surrounded by a family whose interests, both professionally and for enjoyment, were music, there was never a doubt in her mind that she too wanted to become a musician.

She began with classical training through the Suzuki Method and continued into high school majoring primarily in the violin at the School for the Creative and Performing Arts in Cincinnati, OH. Throughout these early years, she also absorbed the sound of a different style of music; bluegrass and fiddling, by the likes of Mark O'Connor, Bela Fleck, and others. Also, while growing up she played in her church ensemble, using her ear to make up her own parts on the spot. By doing this, she developed the desire to improvise and soon got accepted into the jazz program at the University of Cincinnati College-Conservatory of Music, from where she holds a Bachelors Degree.

During her mid-college years, she moved to NYC and gained a lot of performing experience and also attended the New School for Jazz and Contemporary Music in Manhattan. While she was in New York, she received the 2008 Eubie and Marion Blake Award for her achievements in music.

Although violin is her primary instrument, she also enjoys playing the mandolin and singing. Suzanna continues to perform in various styles as well as teach in her hometown of Cincinnati, OH.

Notes

Notes